How to Achieve Better Student Retention in Adult Education

Secrets to becoming an indispensable adult-ed teacher that provides a learning experience that's hard to walk away from (and keeps administrators happy!)

TEDDY EDOUARD

Copyright © 2019 Teddy Edouard
All rights reserved.
ISBN: 978-1-7978-9913-8

DEDICATION

To all the adult-ed teachers, especially those who want to be remarkable ones. And to everyone who is committed to making adult students' lives better. I wrote this book for you.

CONTENTS   PAGES

	Acknowledgments	i
1	Introduction	1
2	Understanding Our Calling	5
3	Taking Matters into Your Own Hands	14
4	Identifying the Warning Signs	20
5	More Than What Students Expected	27
6	Raising Your Learning-Facilitation Game	34
7	Flexible Knowledge and Transferable Skills	44
8	Test Preparation (Game Day!)	51
9	A Real-World Oriented Learning-Facilitation Guidelines	57
10	Conclusion	68

ACKNOWLEDGMENTS

Thank you to my family and to all my friends! You motivate me to get better day by day.

INTRODUCTION

Become the kind of leader that people would follow voluntarily, even if you had no title or position.

— Brian Tracy

Imagine this scenario: You start your semester all excited. Your class (TASC, HiSET, GED, ASE, ABE, ESL, or Workforce) is filled-to-capacity. You labor to choose materials, plan lessons, and get ready for your classes, hoping to keep your adult learners happy.

After a few weeks you realize half your learners have skipped at least one class and several have stopped coming altogether. You know the writing is on the wall.

Things don't look too good, do they?

I have faced this issue several times. My failure was to assume my class was so important that if they really knew what they wanted, the learners just *had* to attend. I worked harder and harder to meet the standards. I made sure learners were aware of the attendance policy.

But that still was not enough to move the needle in the right direction.

Frankly, losing learners made me question my skills as a teacher. I bet it makes you feel the same. But how do you stop the trend of losing learners once it starts? Unfortunately, there is no magic answer to that question. However . . .

The answer may lie in the view we hold of our job and the kind of system we establish to get our adult learners eager for more. Really? Yes, but hold on. I'll elaborate on that a little later.

For now I want to let you know that realistically you may not always be able to maintain a 100 percent retention. That said, your learner attendance rate should not be under 50 percent either, with learners dropping out from your courses like sand through a sieve! Why do I say that? I am glad you asked!

If the bad news is that some learners don't care, the good news is that there are lots of ways to make them care— to motivate and inspire them.

HOW TO ACHIEVE BETTER STUDENT RETENTION

I believe we adult educators have an obligation to inspire our learners to stick around so we can lead them to having better skills and knowledge, and help them solve their learning challenges. But to do so, we have to raise the bar and focus on what matters the most: *helping our learners develop connections and salable skills.*

But first, here are some things to keep in mind before we get deeper into the subject:

- As adult-ed teachers, we work hard. But our work will have little to no impact if we are unable to get learners to come back for more. In other words, we won't see the fruits of our labor unless we get learners to stay until they are changed for the better.

- Learners are in search of "better." Better skills, better connections, and better community. They also have problems they want solved, so they need to learn skills they will use outside the classroom.

- We are leaders and influencers. Thus, we have to lead, influence, empower, and inspire our learners.

- We need learners as much as they need us. A good retention rate is a win-win situation. It keeps our programs in business. Now let's make that even more personal: If your adult education program decides to let go some of its teachers due to budget cuts, will it spare your teaching job? Let that sink in.
- Adult-ed program leaders respect and cherish educators who can keep their learner retention high. These educators are assets no program director wants to lose.

What does all this mean? It means maintaining above-average student retention brings satisfaction to you, your learners, and your program. Everyone wins. But how can you actually make this happen? That is exactly what this retention book is all about.

Like Ryan Holiday puts it, "Wherever we are, whatever we're doing and wherever we are going, we owe it to ourselves, to our art, to the world to do it well."

Warning: If you think you'll get some quick fix in this book, I'm sorry to tell you that you won't find that here. This book does, however, present a philosophy and a process. A system that works, if you can stick to it and are willing to take the risk of trying to be a remarkable adult-ed professional.

Still interested? Great! Then let's start at the beginning by answering this question: Why are you in adult education? In other words, why do you what you do?

CHAPTER 1

Understanding Our Calling

No individual has any right to come into the world and go out of it without leaving behind him distinct and legitimate reasons for having passed through it.

— George Washington Carver

Before we dive into the topic of the retention of learners, let's get our calling straight.

Teaching adult learners to be followers is a lot easier than preparing them to be remarkable. What I mean is that teaching for compliance testing is one of the easiest goals we can meet in adult education. If this is our main priority, we're hiding behind the test instead of leading students to real change.

Most of us adult-ed teachers think our class or lessons are important. So, you might believe learners who really care and are motivated should *of course* attend your classes regularly and abide by the attendance rules. Oh, really? I have news for you.

According Maslow's hierarchy of needs, adult-ed classes are not a basic need. This is my nice way of saying your adult classes are NOT indispensable. But they can become very important if you offer adult learners what they REALLY need and want.

What's that, exactly?

Well, you see—and this is key—adult learners don't want what adult-ed teachers want. They don't like what we like, either. As a matter of fact, adult-ed learners don't even WANT adult-ed classes. What they really need is better reading, writing, speaking, mathematical thinking, and soft skills.

For example, your lessons might seem appealing to YOU, but to learners they might not be appealing at all. They might seem plain and average. What should you do about that? I thought you'd never ask.

The answer is to focus on the true adult-education calling. You might think the calling is preparing adult students for standardized testing. Not quite! Our true calling as adult educators is much more than that. It's about making real change happen so that we make things better for the students we serve.

And by focusing on the true mission of adult education, we are giving learners the very thing they are asking for: a ticket to board the train to success.

This type of calling is not about a learner-teacher relationship of testing and compliance. Instead, it requires a learner-mentor relationship based on trust, choice, and care. In other words, it's about changing students for the better, helping them develop skills they can use in the marketplace.

It's like the familiar adage: Give a man a fish and he eats for a day; teach a man to fish and he eats for a lifetime. We don't want to provide learners with just things they need to pass a test; we want to give them things they can use for the rest of the their lives.

Yes, we adult educators have the ability to make more change than we imagine. And our responsibility is to give learners what they need to succeed on their own in the real world.

In other words, we are called to change our adult students into lifelong learners and help them become the professionals they've dreamed of becoming—or at least to get them closer to where they want to go, one class and one lesson at a time. This might require hard work on a learner's part, but it's a pretty good deal!

As motivational speaker Leo Buscaglia puts it, "Change is the end result of all true learning."

The promise we should make to learners

"The leader is one who, out of the clutter, brings simplicity... out of discord, harmony... and out of difficulty, opportunity."–Albert Einstein

Making the promise to learners that all they need is a degree is misleading. That's because what they *really* need to succeed in the job market, based on the economic trends, is a degree coupled with proven 21st-century skills that are not measured by a test.

Meeting adult students' learning needs is critical to their success in the real world and yours. But you can't meet the needs of learners who dump your class or stop attending your program. So here's the thing: making an impact on your learners starts with your ability to offer them a learning experience that keeps them coming back for more, one class after another.

To be specific, an appealing learning experience for our learners should tap into their passions, desires, and talents. That's why finding a fit between the lessons we teach and what adult students want is so important. Finding that fit will bring more traction to your teaching.

This is where the challenge (or the beauty) comes in. Different learners have different needs and therefore want to go different places. Some don't even know what they want, but they'll know it when they see it. And without a doubt, learners know what progress feels like.

Let me explain. Adult learners are not impressed with average lessons for average students. They want learning that makes them feel good. They want inspiration, leadership, and skills that will help them stand out.

Regardless of the destination each learner wants to reach, our promise to our learners should be to take them on an inspiring learning journey that helps them get closer to their dreams (not the dream we have for them!), one semester at a time.

It's a promise to prepare our adult learners for the real world and facilitate deep-structure learning, promoting soft and irreplaceable skills that are salable in the marketplace or in the gig economy in which freelance jobs are common.

By being consistent in keeping our promise to lead and inspire, we can hope our learners will be compelled to do the same by being consistent in attending classes regularly and on their educational journey.

Making an impact

"The linchpin resists the pressure to conform and comply. Instead, she works without a map, solves interesting problems, leads, connects and creates an impact."—Seth Godin

Every adult-ed teacher has the opportunity to challenge the status quo, encouraging learners to go beyond compliance testing, do art, and be remarkable. But this opportunity comes with a cost. There is a price for leading and teaching in a transformational way—for refusing to be average, fit in, and settle.

In a crowded or traditional adult education field, settling and fitting in is the same as failing—and being average is the same as being invisible. The question is, do you dream of being an invisible adult-ed professional? I don't think so. How do I know? Because you are reading this.

We actually have two options in adult education: be average, invisible, and anonymous, or to take a chance at greatness, uniqueness, and excellence for the sake of the learners who put so much trust in us. What's your choice?

The best way to teach in a transformational way is to not let our expectations of our learners or even of certain learners (that is, our bias about them) get in the way. Instead, set the bar high for all your learners. Promote a race to the top that enables our learners to become proficient in reading, speaking, math, science, or English (depending on the subject you teach), and in teamwork, problem solving, and critical thinking.

Setting the bar high also means pushing students to perform beyond what the test expects or requires of them. Instead, teach for mastery. And the more we teach for mastery and focus on deep-structure learning, the easier the test will look. In other words, the test will take care of itself. The good thing is our work will speak for itself because our learners will show higher order skills across all subject areas.

For example, learners who work to achieve mastery will

- Show the ability to set goals, prioritize, and focus on things that matter

- Read, understand, summarize, and present all kinds of texts, both orally and in writing

- Express themselves with tact publicly and ask pertinent questions

- Read between the lines and make inferences

- Show agency and the ability to learn new things on their own

HOW TO ACHIEVE BETTER STUDENT RETENTION

- Use the appropriate frame of reference to approach math problems and scientific information produced for a variety of contexts or situations

- Demonstrate an ability to understand and use abstract conceptualization, information, evidence, and data to make generalizations

- Think critically, approaching and solving complex problems with a growth mindset

- Connect classroom learning and skills to real-world situations and discuss current trends

- Show emotional intelligence and self-control during discussions

- Develop soft and irreplaceable skills and competencies

- Develop and explore their talents

Systems win championships

"I think leadership is service and there is power in that giving: to help people, to inspire and motivate them to reach their fullest potential." – Denise Morrison

A player's success is almost always guaranteed under Coach Bill Belichick, head coach of The New England Patriots. He is known for his ability to transform average NFL players into Super Bowl champs. How? Season after season, he uses a system that almost always works.

Coach Belichick was once mentored by Bill Parcells. Coach Parcells is also known for his ability to change dysfunctional NFL teams into a winning machine. These two men have one great quality in common: they know how to build a system that inspires people.

Frank Robinson also had a system. He won consistently. He became the only player to earn the Most Valuable Player award in both the National Baseball League and the American Baseball League. Impressive, isn't it? This wasn't luck. His system worked in Cincinnati and in Baltimore. And guess what? He became the first black manager in baseball major league history.

So, what are YOU known for?

I've used the examples above just to show that there's a big difference between telling learners they need to attend classes and instilling a learning desire in them. There's a big difference in teaching them what they need to know for the test and piquing their curiosity, creating in them a thirst for knowledge or the desire for becoming better day by day. And we must use our passion and ideas to inspire students as opposed to using attendance rules or requirements to just manage them.

That's why teachers should create systems that work. As adult-ed educators, we can build a system far bigger than ourselves. A system that will keep learners coming back for more and set students on the path to proficiency. Just like with athletes playing for a good coach, our learners will realize what we are trying to achieve and will be willing to follow if we are ready to lead them.

In other words, focus on teaching for real change. To quote marketing guru Seth Godin, "Paint a picture of the future. Go there. People will follow."

CHAPTER 2

Taking Matters into Your Own Hands

Do not follow where the path may lead. Go instead where there is no path and leave a trail.

— *Ralph Waldo Emerson*

Now, it may be that your program doesn't have a clear student retention system. But that's no excuse not to have your own system. Having a system that works is the first step in keeping your promise to change learners for the better, leading them to intellectual growth.

When it comes to student retention, program administrators' influence is limited; they can't do as much as you are able to. So, this gives YOU the opportunity to come in to save the day (or the semester!). It's up to you to use your influence.

HOW TO ACHIEVE BETTER STUDENT RETENTION

Remember, for your learners, you are the ultimate learning guide, facilitator, and the leader. Why do I say that? Because you shape their classroom and learning experience. As a result, most learners might decide to stay in class because of what you do—and what you offer them.

In other words, your interactions with learners matter. How you make them feel is important! The environment you create in your classroom counts. The progress they make under your leadership is critical; their learning, in major part, depends on how you interact with your students.

Now the key question is this: Do you have a system that focuses on learners' needs?

Remember, you can't be a teacher without learners. You don't have a job without them! So your success as a teacher is dependent on their achievements under your guidance.

Therefore, student retention is a factor in your teaching career that you should control as much as you can. We all know we can't control what's happening in students' lives outside of our classroom. But you CAN be a leader they want to follow. You can inspire them to come back to the classroom for more learning regardless of the challenges they face outside of it.

Students' learning in your classroom setting falls under your jurisdiction. So, don't leave anything to chance! Offer students a learning experience that's hard to walk away from because it helps them get better each day.

In other words, give them *more* than they think they need. Give them transferable skills, structure, agency, critical thinking, connections, and—above all—community and inspiration.

But let's be frank: this is harder than it sounds! But I know you want to do it for the sake of your learners. But how? You can start by telling them the truth.

The lies that stand in the way

"All of the great leaders have had one characteristic in common: it was the willingness to confront unequivocally the major anxiety of their people in their time. This, and not much else, is the essence of leadership." – John Kenneth Galbraith

Most of your learners are afraid of failure, blame, and criticism. Are you able to see the fear in their eyes? Unless you are well aware of their fear, you won't be able to help them "dance" with it. What do I mean?

I mean you have to teach your learners how to face their fear and embrace it. Just like in ballroom dancing, you face your partner and embrace him or her. The first time you did this, especially if you were young, you were probably nervous and a bit afraid. You worried you'd get out there on the dance floor and mess up. But after a while, you realized you could do it and you enjoyed it. Perhaps you even wondered why you'd even been fearful in the first place.

It's the same with teaching your students to face their fear and embrace it so they can reach success after trying and maybe some practice. Teaching your students to dance with their fear might be the most important skill you will ever teach in your career.

What I'm saying is that adult-ed professionals have a responsibility to tell their students the truth. What truth? Let me explain.

Most adult-ed students have been exposed to a lot of lies about learning, such as how people learn, what makes people smart, and what they are able to learn or not able to learn. So, your best teaching move might be to help students adopt a growth mindset. How? By addressing the lies and discussing the difference between a growth and a fixed mindset.

Let's tackle some of the lies, one by one:

Lie #1: You can raise your hand only if you have the correct answer or something smart to say.
Reaction: As Seth Godin puts it, "It's OK to be wrong on the way to being right."

Lie #2: Don't ask stupid questions.
Reaction: See Lie #1!

Lie #3: Students who complete their work quickly are smart.
Reaction: When it comes to learning, the process is as important as the product. Thus, students should take the time to think deeply about content. Remember that the classroom is not the Olympic Games!

Lie #4: Don't speak if you don't know what you're talking about.
Reaction: This is misleading because students won't know if they are wrong unless they share their ideas.

Lie #5: You should get everything right the first time (if you're smart).
Reaction: Learning takes time. People who say they got it the first time might be pretending or faking it. Time will tell!

Lie #6: STEM is not for everyone.
Reaction: Really, who has the right to say that? Students just need a teacher who can open their eyes and mind to the STEM

world. The truth is, students can learn whatever they want as long as they are willing to put in the work and the effort.

Lie #7: Having good grades means you are smart.
Reaction: In the marketplace, everything comes down to skills and competencies. No employer asks about grades during an interview (unless the employer is a nut!).

Lie #8: Students with high test scores are smart.
Reaction: See point # 7. As noted educator Dr. Carol Dweck puts it, "Test scores and measures of achievement tell you where a student is, but they don't tell you where a student could end up."

Lie #9: If you don't have a high IQ, you're not smart.
Reaction: In my opinion, the IQ test is a joke. For example, most people would agree Albert Einstein had a very high IQ; he was a genius. But most people fail to recognize that Einstein studied a lot and worked hard to accomplish what he did. He published 450 papers, but he did not just magically write the papers. He had to work at it.

Lie #10: You need to go with the flow. Do your best to fit in. Be like the other students.
Reaction: Fitting in is a sure way to be invisible and fail in the marketplace.

Lie #11: Whatever is not on the test is not important, so don't worry about it.

Reaction: Students SHOULD worry about it. Students should learn for the real world, not just for a test. Learning never stops. It does not end with the standardized test.

Addressing these lies send a clear message that adult education is not a punishment but a way and a place where learners can become better day by day.

The shame-proof classroom

"I've learned that people will forget what you said, people will forget what you did, but people will never forget how you made them feel." – Maya Angelou

Shame is a bad feeling. Nobody likes it. And your learners are no exception. Learners won't keep coming back to a classroom where they experience shame and embarrassment.

Therefore, learners need a space free of shame and embarrassment—a space that's welcoming and conducive to real-world learning. Your ability to create this mistake-friendly environment where learners can thrive is indispensable to their learning success.

CHAPTER 3

Identifying the Warning Signs

A leader is one who sees more than others see, who sees farther than others see, and who sees before others see.

— Leroy Eimes

Can you tell when a learner is about to give up and walk away? Being able to see the warning signs of someone who's about to give up allows you to reach out to these learners, providing them with just-in-time support. Reaching them in time is all about being proactive.

An adult learner doesn't ditch a class (TASC, HiSET, GED, ASE, ABE, ESL or Workforce) suddenly and without warning. Rather, he or she makes up his or her mind gradually. But as an instructor, are you able to see the warning signs?

Being able to identify the signs allows you to reach out to learners, providing the support and assurance they might need to stay in class. It's all about being proactive, like a lifeguard constantly watching the swimmers to make sure none are floundering. You're the sheepdog that constantly watches the flock for signs of trouble or danger.

The secret is, most adult learners think twice before giving up on a teacher who cares about them. But how do you show them you really care (if you really do)? I will get to that shortly...

To support your teaching efforts, let me share a few examples of warning signs with you. These signs might tell you if a learner is getting ready, consciously or unconsciously, to dump your class. Shall we dive in?

1. Too many unexcused absences

Adult learners who miss too many classes might feel they will never catch up with their classmates. That brings them the shame and embarrassment I mentioned earlier. Thus, they will leave your class.

What to do about it:

- Reach out to learners with many absences. Let them know you care and you are concerned about their progress/learning.

- Address absences and offer help (only things you can actually help with, of course).

- Review expectations and provide extra support.

- Help students leave the class gracefully so they can come back if they want to.

- Don't make them feel judged.

It's critical to let students know you understand their situation and want to help them get back on track.

2. Cell phone use

Learners who are constantly on the phone talking and texting during class time have other commitments (or distractions) and know they are breaking the rules. Breaking the rules brings shame and embarrassment, causing students to leave once this embarrassment is too much to bear.

What to do about it:

- Have a conversation about the issue but don't come across as accusatory or condemning.

- Review expectations.

- Discuss potential solutions to the issues and provide accommodation as necessary.

- Help students leave the class gracefully if they really have to so they can come back later when and if they are able to.

3. Lack of participation and engagement

This is a critical one. Disengaged learners don't stay in class for long and why should they?

When learners are not engaged in the learning process, they don't retain the information taught in class. Not learning is a waste of their time. As a result, they will bid you *adieu* as soon as they find something more interesting to do.

What to do about it:

- Make sure learners know you are concerned about their participation.

- Get to know learners' interests (what they like to do).

- Make your teaching relevant to their needs. Help learners see the big picture (the connection between concepts and skills).

- Develop and facilitate learning activities that involve all learners.

- Allow the space and time for all learners to think and collaborate.

- Use a variety of pair-work and group work to get everyone involved.

- Discuss students' work and progress weekly or biweekly.

- Minimize downtime since learners have a hard time picking up speed and motivation after periods of downtime.

- Reflect on progress during every single class so learners can see and intentionally think about their efforts and learning.

This book addresses the issue of learners' lack of engagement in more detail in Chapters 4 and 5.

4. No personal connection

"This idea of shared humanity and the connections that we make with one another - that's what, in fact, makes life worth living."— Clint Smith

With no classroom connections (or friends) face major challenges. For example, they struggle to take risks, to talk about their real needs, and to be real with strangers. In other words, they feel too vulnerable.

HOW TO ACHIEVE BETTER STUDENT RETENTION

Maslow's hierarchy of needs might help you better understand why personal connection is important to your learners. I strongly encourage you to read more about this hierarchy.

Connecting learners with fellow classmates that face the same struggles will make things make the student feel better. Learners need to know they are not the only ones struggling in the learning process.

What to do about it:

- Run the class like a community (and let learners share responsibility).

- Create activities that build and reinforce the community structure, especially at the beginning of the class term.

- Get to know your learners and what motivates them.

- Encourage learners to work and study together in groups.

- Check on students both in groups and individually on regular basis and listen to their concerns.

- Be intentional about providing time and space for learners to socialize.

- Implement group work and small group projects from day one.

Above all, learners need to know they can trust you. I will tackle this issue in more detail in Chapters 4 and 5.

Keep in mind that dealing with adult learners' emotions is an important task that an adult-ed instructor needs to do well. My advice to you: don't miss or ignore the warning signs of a student about to drop your class. Keep an open line of communication and deal with your learners with the utmost respect and consideration.

You never know. You may become the only motivation your learners have to attend classes regularly.

CHAPTER 4

More Than What Students Expected

A good objective of leadership is to help those who are doing poorly to do well and to help those who are doing well to do even better.

— Jim Rohn

When it comes to learner retention, goals are overrated. They barely work. Shocking, right? What you need is to establish a system that makes learners feel they belong and drives effective learning.

A system that

- Builds community
- Helps learners build connections
- Gives learners a voice
- Makes learners feel safe
- Gives them a desire to learn

Further, learners need to also be taught how to build their own systems. For example, they need a system that helps them

- Come to class regularly and on time
- Study or work with classmates
- Practice independently
- Take care of all aspects of their lives

As author Scott Adams says, a system is better than a bunch of goals.

For example, you should establish a support system that works for all learners, just like Coach Belichick does for all his players. This may take time, but it gives learners a sense of belonging (Maslow's hierarchy of needs). This might be the draw that will keep them coming back.

Let's face it. Losing learners week after week is demoralizing for both you and the rest of your class. But things can get even worse. How?

The more learners you lose, the higher the potential you will lose more. That's because of the domino effect. This is why you must stop this trend early!

Keeping adult learners interested in your class requires more than teaching content—it takes a holistic approach. I personally find it difficult to keep all my learners interested. But I've never given up on a learner!

And guess what? Over the years I've developed a system for my classes and my coaching work that maximizes student engagement and retention. Let's go over some interventions you can add to your system, regardless of the subject you teach.

HOW TO ACHIEVE BETTER STUDENT RETENTION

1. Raise awareness about why your class is important

Your learners may not know why they should study your content. So, it's your responsibility to pitch your subject to them. List the specific skills your learners will be able to develop and they can apply in the real world. Explain how you will help them ace the standardized test.

Then use stories, concrete examples, visuals, and your sense of humor to get and keep the students' attention. Don't be too formal, plain, and boring. Rather, be approachable and relatable—this is adult-ed, remember?

Give your learners a reason to trust you, to study the content you present, and to come back to your class. Invite them to commit to the learning journey and keep your end of the bargain, too.

2. Create a classroom community

"Setting the emotional climate for learning may be the most important task a teacher embarks on each day." Dr. Mariale M. Hardiman

Forget about teaching for a moment. Rather, work on building community. Encourage connections. Employ get-to-know-you activities so you can learn about your students and they can learn about each other. Work at connecting with your learners on a personal level. Have conversations. Show learners you care. Listen to your students' stories.

Create space for learners to mingle with each other to talk about expectations, fears, and challenges.

Plan to establish a support system for learners. This may take time, but it gives learners a sense of belonging. (Here we go again with Maslow's hierarchy of needs!) You never know—this sense of belonging might be the very thing that keeps your learners coming back.

3. Teach time management

Regardless of the focus of your class, teaching or reviewing good time management tips is critical to your learners' success. How do I address this?

Here are some ways:

- Have a conversation about the benefits of keeping a schedule or an agenda (a system).

- Share time management tools (templates, smartphones tips) that enable learners to plan their daily and weekly schedules.

- Help students develop a schedule for the whole class term.

- Show learners how to prioritize life events and tasks.

- Encourage learners to block out time to study, read, and practice.

Consider encouraging learners to study or work with friends, classmates, or family members that will hold them accountable.

Having someone to hold them accountable can help motivate them to stay on track.

4. Keep an open line of communication

"Communication is the most important skill any leader can possess." – Richard Branson

Establish a class communication system. Keep your system simple, consistent, and easy.
Here's how:

- Discuss your communication expectations with learners. This includes expectations about absence and lateness notifications.

- Have students contribute to a notification policy for absences and tardiness.

- Set up and send out group reminders as necessary (texts, Google voice, or emails).

- Discuss attendance policy and expectations with your class (such as the minimum hours required for post-testing).

- Provide learners with tools to help them keep track of their attendance, if necessary.

- Use group texts, calls (Google voice), emails and other relevant media to keep learners informed and connected.

- During class, call or text learners who are skipping the class. Why? Because it's the perfect time to let them know their absence is noticeable.
- Reach out to learners who are missing classes and use your personal connection with them as leverage. (But don't come across as judgmental.)

Use communication to foster good rapport with your class. Listen to your learners. Understand them. Treating them with utmost respect will show you genuinely care.

5. Have a clear classroom structure (routines)

It will help your learners if they know what to expect, what to do, and how to find the materials they need. Take guesswork out of your classroom setting. Be predictable. Use clear classroom routines and frameworks.

Here's how:

- Set clear performance objectives or goals for the class.

- Have a clear syllabus for the class term and go over it with the learners. Let them make suggestions.

- Start and end your class on time.

- Be intentional when starting and closing your lesson. Avoid having students walk away with no sense of closure.

- Have a clear agenda that the class can refer to from time to time during lesson implementation and get your learners' input on their readiness to transition to new stages.
- Show clear transitions from one unit to the next.

- Teach learners to organize their work and your handouts (use physical, online binders, or folders).

- Give homework regularly (if appropriate for your teaching context).

- Have a clear strategy to bring absentees up to speed and let learners know what they should do to catch up after missing a class.

A clear structure or a system will help learners develop productive study and work habits. However, be mindful that some learners may need extra support, so expect to differentiate your strategies and routines. The next chapter covers some critical aspects of lesson implementation. See you there!

CHAPTER 5

Raising Your Learning-Facilitation Game

For most of us the problem isn't that we aim too high and fail—it's just the opposite—we aim too low and succeed.

— *Sir Ken Robinson*

No matter what you teach (math, science, social studies, ESL, or RELA), your learner retention rate will, for the most part, depend on the learning experience you offer your students.

Like me, you've had many teachers in your lifetime. But how many of their classes would you be happy to attend again if you could? I am sure you wouldn't choose to sit through any of the dreadful, boring, or dull classroom experiences.

HOW TO ACHIEVE BETTER STUDENT RETENTION

Similarly, have you ever wondered how your learners feel about your classes? Would they want to stay with you if they are given other options?

Let's explore a few teaching techniques that can be critical to keeping learners engaged in the learning process—and committed to your classes.

1. Do more than just teach a class—create an active-learning experience

Have you ever heard of LX? It stands for "learner experience." It's a big deal in the corporate world and in Silicon Valley. You should adapt the principles of the LX into your adult-ed classroom. Leveraging the LX is good teaching practice. It works.

No matter what you teach, your learner retention rate will, for the most part, depend on how your classroom experience makes learners feel. As a result, your teaching practices should tap into learners' minds, brains, feelings, and emotions.

How? Let's go over some strategies:

- Put your learners in situations where they have to respond, manipulate, and react to class content. Allow them to bring examples and their own their personal experiences into the lessons.

- Give learners a voice and encourage them to use it.

- Value learners' contributions to lessons. This helps tap into learners' schemas.

- "Storify" your content by presenting your content in the form of stories, and create space for learners to interact with the stories.

- Use scenarios, concrete examples, and discussions that mimic reality—especially your learners' reality.

- Differentiate your instructions by aligning your content to various learners' needs and interests.

- Develop and improve learners' transferable skills (critical thinking, presentation, group work, public speaking, note-taking, reading comprehension, and writing). Encourage them to apply the learning immediately in their context.

- Implement student-centered teaching approaches that tackle key standards and skills.

- Apply good classroom management techniques to establish a secure atmosphere and a productive learning environment that makes students take more risks.

- Help students reflect on their learning, its applications, and implications, thereby making their progress visible.

- Have regular conversations about what's going well in the class and what needs to change or be adjusted.

2. Teach how to learn, unlearn and relearn

"The illiterate of the 21st century will not be those who cannot read and write, but those who cannot learn, unlearn, and relearn." — *Alvin Toffler*

Students who use metacognitive skills—that is, understand how they learn and use techniques to enhance their learning—are way ahead of the game.

Do you like to sit through long lectures? I bet you don't. And your learners don't either. Let's put it another way. What's your ratio of teacher talk time to student talk time? If you speak too much, chances are you you're not empowering your learners. That is, referring to the earlier analogy, you are giving them the fish instead of teaching them how to fish.

Teaching students how to learn is empowering and sets them on the path to autonomy. How do I do that?

Here's what you can do:

- Show learners how to find and access class content.

- Teach study skills, strategies, and the best ways to handle class content.

- Provide appropriate resources and sources.

- Use teaching practices or activities that promote learners' autonomy.

- Create opportunity for distributed and meaningful practices.

- Keep learners on tasks and challenge their assumptions.

- Make room for presentations and add academic rigor to the presentation process.

- Flip the class, if possible, encouraging students to go over content before coming to class. And provide independent study time or review time.

- Implement pair-work and group work as often as possible. This will promote peer learning.

- Use guiding and follow-up questions and let learners do the same.

- Create room for debates and discussions. This will allow learners to articulate and clarify their thoughts and opinions.

- Help learners create tangible and meaningful products and time the learning tasks.

- Discuss standards with learners and encourage them reflect on their progress towards meeting the expectations.

- Show learners the big picture. Use visuals to describe what they will be working on for the chapter or lesson. And help them connect current learning activities to previously taught materials.

- Use guidelines and frameworks, such as the Universal Design for Learning (UDL), The Brain-Targeted Teaching Model (BTT), Presentation–Practice–Production (PPP/U), Pre-During-Post (PDP), or the 5E instructional model to foster a rigorous, structured learning environment and promote learners' autonomy.

3. Celebrate effort over talent

"Hard work beats talent when talent fails to work hard." — Kevin Durant

Talent is overrated. Let's face it, at some point, most adult learners have struggled with low self-esteem. Before taking your class, past learning experiences may have prevented them from doing their best. This is where you come in to elevate them! Shifting the focus from being smart to being hard-working will encourage students to step up and do more.

Having a conversation about the superiority of hard work over talent is critical to a learner's success. In other words, do your best to give feedback when learners show effort, determination, resilience, and tenacity.

Make even small progress visible to learners, and provide them with constructive, corrective feedback so they can fix their mistakes and improve their work. And don't forget to applaud mistakes for having the courage to try.

How can you do that? Here are some ways:

- Welcome mistakes and leverage them to help learners improve their skills. Avoid chasing correct answers. Instead, focus on process.

- Provide specific feedback on completed tasks. Praise efforts.

- Encourage learners to keep a portfolio—a collection of works or achievements—so they can monitor and see their improvement.

- Celebrate leadership and responsibility.

- Praise good time-management efforts.

- Praise decision-making skills and critical thinking.

- Value collaborative skills.

- Encourage group work skills.

- Celebrate a positive outlook and attitude.

- Do regular check-ins with learners, and address challenges or concerns that might stand in the way.

The bottom line is to focus on creating learning experiences that elevate your learners rather than diminishes them as people.

4. Build factual knowledge

We both can agree it's hard to get learners to think critically. Why? Because It's a human thing. For instance, research in cognitive science shows the brain is not very good at thinking (shocking!). Rather, it's better at protecting learners from having to think. Really...? Trust me, I couldn't make that up.

Wait...there's more! Students can't think critically without having the appropriate background or factual knowledge. What does that really mean? Keep on reading...

"The very processes that teachers care about most—critical thinking processes such as reasoning and problem solving—are intimately intertwined with factual knowledge that is stored in long-term memory," says the cognitive scientist and author Daniel Willingham. That is to say, your students will learn and think better if they have some background knowledge about the content or subject you teach.

For example, doing reading, science, ESL, or math work that shows the learner no sign he or she is making progress is not pleasurable. It can be extremely frustrating. On the other hand, giving students a tasks with easy-to-find, obvious answers brings no sense of achievement and satisfaction.

I'd suggest cognitive tasks that introduce new challenges by building on what students already know how to do. Use videos or stories to activating prior knowledge and provide background information before students read about key content. Go over concepts or words that will help students access the content. And use controversial questions that require students to bring their personal opinion to the table.

The bottom line is to focus on creating learning experiences that elevate your learners rather than diminishes them as people.

5- Leverage learners' curiosity

During a closing statement at a workshop on improving the quality of adult teaching, I said this: "Finding the correct answer, answering obvious questions, filling in the blanks are all boring activities —and stand in the way of effective student learning."

A participant from the back of the conference room quickly raised her hand and said, "How about the tests? Don't we have to prepare our learners for these tests?"

liked the question. It's a classic one that I almost always get when I speak about using engaging teaching practices in adult education. Now you must be curious to know how I answered it. Aren't you? Here was my response:

I have yet to meet an adult student that is dying to take a standardized test because the content and the questions were so interesting. It's obvious adult learners want to do well on these tests, but they aren't crazy about the questions per se.

It's true, helping learners ace a test is the sine qua none of effective teaching. However, adult-ed teachers who want to prepare students for the test in a traditional kind of way—with worksheets and quizzes—run the risk of being very boring. And the outcome? Almost no learners left to test at the end of the semester!

But the most important thing I said was this: We prepare students for the test while keeping them interested in attending classes. How? By exploiting their curiosity. Why? Let me explain...

Adult students might not like to think critically because it's hard. But they are all curious. How do I know? It's human nature! For instance, the cognitive scientist, Dr. Daniel Willingham, put it this way: "People are naturally curious, but we are not naturally good thinkers; unless the cognitive conditions are right, we will avoid thinking."

To tap into curiosity, we need to avoid using obvious questions and chasing correct answers. Rather, piquing student's curiosity forces them to think about and engage with the content in a deeper way—which leads to better information retention for the test.

Learners have the desire to understand, to try, to seek out what's coming next—but this desire needs to be activated. Once they get a whiff of what's cooking in the kitchen, they'll get hungry. Imagine having a group of students that can't wait to start the next lesson.

6- Make storytelling work for you

The secret to teaching classes that learners will comprehend and remember is to organize the whole lesson— from beginning to end— like a good story. For example, running your lesson like a story should be like creating an episode of popular and intriguing TV show. In other words, imbed important concepts, key information, and instructions in well-crafted stories. Doing so will make your content intriguing and unforgettable.

"But how do I organize my lesson like a story?" Great question. I almost forgot to share what makes a story interesting. Let's get to it now. A compelling story has the following ingredients:

1. casualty
2. conflict
3. complication
4. characters
5. action
6. and uses a simple And-But-Therefore formula.

Using these ingredients and formula might make your lesson memorable? Memorable? Yes. I am not kidding. Here's the thing, from the beginning of time storytelling has always been captivating for the human mind. For example, research in cognitive science argued, "The human mind seems exquisitely tuned to understand and remember stories." So, why not taking advantage of storytelling to better hook your students' attention?

CHAPTER 6

Flexible Knowledge and Transferable Skills

The gardener does not make a plant grow. The job of a gardener is to create optimal conditions.

— Sir Ken Robinson

OK, now that you've retained most of your learners, let's discuss how we can promote deeper learning. Effective learning should be the ultimate outcome of your teaching and should be at the heart of your learner-retention interventions and strategies. Keep in mind, our calling in adult education is to prepare students for the real world not just for compliance testing.

For example, your system should create proficient learners in your content. On top of that, learners should be able to demonstrate speaking and thinking skills.

But the real question is, what level of knowledge do you want learners to develop? Being able to answer that question will enable you to choose your teaching activities carefully. So, why let's take a look at what I mean by levels of knowledge:

1. Rote knowledge

Rote knowledge is superficial. It's about memorizing and repeating factual information. Therefore, learners might be able to use or repeat rote knowledge without understanding its meaning, implication, and application.

Don't let your students remain at this stage! Rather, take them to the next level. Take learning deeper and make learners work on meaningful learning tasks.

2. Inflexible knowledge

New knowledge is inflexible and volatile. It is not effective learning, but it is better than rote knowledge. It's like the first runner up in a spelling bee: it's better, but not the very best.

According to cognitive scientist Dr. Daniel Willingham, inflexible knowledge is a level of learning that allows students to perform tasks only in known contexts or the settings where the knowledge was learned. It's not deep enough to be transferred to other contexts. Again, we still need to reinforce this kind of learning.

How? By using distributed practice activities that reflect the real world. These activities also can enable your students to form flexible knowledge. What is flexible knowledge? Good question! The next section provides the answer.

3. Flexible knowledge

According to research in cognitive science, flexible knowledge is a higher order of learning. It involves the understanding of form, meaning, implications, and applications. Most importantly, it leads to the development and reinforcement of critical thinking skills.

Learners acquire flexible knowledge by using effective learning principles: that is, by using meaningful and distributed practices. When learners acquire flexible knowledge, they are able to apply it in a variety of contexts, including during test taking and in the real world.

 other words, this knowledge is transferable because it is rooted and resides in what the cognitive scientists called deep-structure learning. What do I mean by deep-structure learning? Allow me to explain.

Deep structure, according to Dr. Willingham, is when learners achieve transferable learning and skills that can be used in a variety of contexts. It's the ability to understand and use abstract conceptualization and generalization to make appropriate decisions. It encompasses critical thinking and problem solving skills.

It's challenging to reach deep-structure learning, but you can help students do it. How? By focusing on cognitive tasks, real-world examples, and experiences that allow students to transform inflexible learning into flexible knowledge. The more students do tasks that promote deep-structure learning, the better they will be at transferring their knowledge to different real life situations.

For instance, some of the teaching approaches that can lead to this level of learning are case-based learning, project-based learning, problem-based learning, and experiential learning. Let's take a closer look at each of them.

Case-Based learning

This approach allows adult-ed instructors to create opportunities for learners to use critical thinking and analytical skills to work in groups or in pairs on real world challenges. Mastering CBL implementation might take time; but working on this skill is worth every minute you spend on it.

I am not lying, being a proficient user of this approach will elevate you to the rank of top learning facilitators in the adult-ed field. Wouldn't you like that?

But wait a minute. Where do I find the cases? You can either learn to write your own cases or find them in books or on the internet. Let's look at the second approach.

Project-based learning

Like Case-Based Learning, project-based learning activities mimic the real world. It allows learners to spend a few classes or even a term solving meaningful and complex problems for a real audience.

Now you are wondering: What kind of projects should your learners work on? They should do work that is aligned with the core standards and learning objectives they are trying to reach.

For example, you should use PBL guidelines and frameworks that can get your learners to put their understanding and skills in evidence. That said, being able to showcase real products that your learners create will make them feel and look good. Isn't it rewarding for them?

Problem-based learning

The Problem-Based Learning model allows adult-ed teachers to foster classroom collaboration, allowing learners to show critical thinking skills and creativity. That is, learners work on open-ended problems that require the utilization of skills aligned with learning objectives set for the class. Applying the PBL principles will make you look distinguished.

But I already know what you are thinking: How the heck is problem-based learning different from project-based learning? Well, you are right. They are close cousins. But… simply put, many consider problem-based learning as a subcategory of project-based learning.

For example, problem-based learning can be implemented in a short period of time vs project-based learning that calls for more resources and a more extended period of time.

Experiential Learning

This approach may tap into the approaches I described above to take learners through a learning cycle. Adult ed instructors often use it to expose learners to experiences outside the classroom setting. The phases of experiential learning includes: Concrete Experience, Reflective Observation, Abstract Conceptualization, and Active Experimentation. In other words, this teaching approach is all about learning by doing and reflecting.

The bottom line is, being proficient in all the 4 teaching approaches is ideal. But mastering one approach is all you need for now. Like I said before, facilitating learning like a pro is a win-win situation for you and your learners— they learn better and you look better (professionally).

A note about automaticity

Developing flexible knowledge—that is, mastering content and skills—involves information processing and complex mental tasks, such as reading, thinking, and analyzing, to name a few. Unfortunately, learners who do not master basic skills and basic information in the adult-ed classroom tend to struggle to do higher-order thinking and mental tasks.

My point is, for learners to reach deep-structure learning and complete mental tasks successfully, they must first reach "automaticity" in their use of basic skills, information, and procedures related to the content.

As Dr. Willingham says, "Automaticity is vital in education because it allows us to become more skillful in mental tasks."

So, what can we do to promote automaticity in our students? We can plan regular, consistent, distributed practice sessions that enable student to work on foundational skills and procedures until they reach

automaticity. Reaching automaticity will ensure their success when dealing with more complex mental activities in the adult-ed classroom.

For example, your learners will do better in

- Dealing with math problems if they've reached automaticity in doing basic operations, the order of operations, and key mathematical concepts

- Accessing scientific texts if they've reached automaticity in recalling basic factual knowledge and understanding key concepts or terminology

- Reading different types of texts if they've reached automaticity in knowing how to read for comprehension (that is, able to identify the main idea, details, the author's intent, and clues about context)

- Reading English if they've reached automaticity in recalling factual knowledge and the ESL lexis that relates to the content at hand

Allow me to quote Dr. Willingham to cement my point: "...procedures must be learned to the point of automaticity so that they no longer consume working memory space." In other words, your students will be able to think better and faster if they master basic skills to the point that they can recall them automatically.

CHAPTER 7

Test Preparation (Game Day!)

Language-lovers know that there is a word for every fear. Are you afraid of wine? Then you have oenophobia. Tremulous about train travel? You suffer from siderodromophobia. Having misgivings about your mother-in-law is pentheraphobia, and being petrified of peanut butter sticking to the roof of your mouth is arachibutyrophobia. And then there's Franklin Delano Roosevelt's affliction, the fear of fear itself, or phobophobia.

— *Steven Pinker*

That leads us to *testophobia*. Get ready to help some of your learners to manage it.

After covering deeper learning in the previous sections, are you ready to dive into the preparation tips for standardized testing? OK, then let's get started!

I waited so long to write about testing because, let's face it, if your students can reach mastery or flexible knowledge, testing will take care of itself. But even with strong skills and knowledge, students need to learn to perform under pressure.

It is a fact that some of your learners might not perform well under testing pressure. Thus, your class should start training on the very first day of class. Be sure to have your students perform under the pressure of the test at least every other week. By the time they take the final test, their brain will have gotten used to its intensity.

Covering key standards (Common Core, Next Generation Science Standards, EL Proficiency Standards, GED Standards, NRS, TABE, CASAS, and College & Career Readiness) in your lessons is a good thing, but it's not enough to lead students to perform well on standardized tests. Why? Your students need to also know the test instructions, format, timing and structure—and know them very well.

The bad news is learners who do not perform well on the tests might get discouraged and leave your class or program. This is demoralizing for both you and your learners, isn't it? But the good news is you can almost always avoid this pitfall by teaching for mastery and helping learners to know the test inside and out.

Here are a few useful ways to help students prepare for taking tests:

1. Write learner-centered learning objectives

Set learning objectives (LOs) instead of using coverage objectives (COs). COs are about the content you and your institution want to cover in the class. But we both know these COs won't necessarily lead to effective learning, don't we?

That's why writing LOs is the way to go. They indicate what skills and competencies your students should be able to learn and do at the end of your lesson. Your LOs should reflect real-world, authentic experiences. As a result, your learners are likely do better on the test. Why?

Why? As Dr. Willingham puts it, "The brain stores most information in the form of meaning." Therefore, meaningful learning experiences will facilitate students' learning and information retention.

2. Distribute your practice sessions

As I said before, avoiding massed practices or cramming is key. Not only is making students practice lots of materials at once too cumbersome, and it simply does not work—nor does it improve performance on the test.

Rather, distributing your practice sessions as much possible across several weeks works better. And planning homework assignments and classwork accordingly further will enable learners to revisit class materials throughout the term.
This will also be an opportunity to recycle content and to practice managing *testophobia*, using some mindfulness techniques.

Most importantly, research shows distributed practices can help get students better prepared to face standardized tests. In other words, the spacing effect will work in your and your students' favor. (Yes, the spacing effect is a thing!)

Let's briefly address the importance and benefits of practice. Practice is what exercise is for your body. As psychologist Daniel Willingham puts it, "It is virtually impossible to become proficient at a mental task without extended practice."

In other words, practice (or guided learning) is helpful in numerous ways.

For instance, it

- Helps develop and reinforce new skills
- Prevents us from forgetting recently learned information and skills
- Facilitates knowledge transfer for the long run
- Makes thinking processes automatic
- Reinforces memory
- Transforms surface knowledge into deep-structure learning

From a cognitive science perspective, learners practice well when they are intentional in what they do.

For example, they need to

- Get and use effective feedback to fix mistakes and improve on skills
- Focus on improving specific skills or how to effectively learn new skills
- Reflect on their progress and decide how to move forward accordingly

By the way, effective feedback might motivate your learners. It is like fuel that keeps their learning-engine running.

Here's what makes feedback effective:

1. **Timely:** It's immediate and fresh. It is given soon after the work has been completed.
2. **Corrective:** It points to specific issues that need fixing. Therefore, it suggests how to improve the work.
3. **Criterion-based:** It tells learners how they are doing as it relates to a specific standards, goal, or rubric they are supposed to meet.
4. **Student-facilitated:** It allows learners to have a voice in the process. They are given a chance to articulate their specific needs or weaknesses and request appropriate help.

Specifically speaking, if learners get no feedback on their assignments, their coming to class and the work they do really mean nothing—it's like flying a plane with no radar and no guidance from the control tower. The bottom line is, make effective feedback an integral part of all your practice sessions.

3. Teach study skills and strategies for THE TEST

Using effective study skills makes learners more confident, and their confidence improves even more when they are consistent in their studies.

For example, 30 minutes of study a day over 15 weeks is way better than 20 hours of study just before the final test.

That is to say, your learners should practice regularly. The spacing effect will give them a better grip of the class materials, helping them to be better prepared by the time they have to take the test.

Repeated practice is by far the best remedy against forgetfulness. To quote educational psychologist Dr. Daniel Willingham,

"Anticipating the effect of forgetting dictates that we continue our practice beyond the mastery we desire."

Similarly, learners need to practice and connect new material with old ones. Doing so regularly will help adult students create long-lasting knowledge and memory. Isn't that what we all want? As Dr. Willingham says, "As teachers, we want long-lasting knowledge, not just knowledge for a few days."

Good performance on standardized tests is like adding fuel to the fire of learners' motivation. The better they do, the more they want to learn—and the more persistent they become about learning. And isn't that what you and your adult-ed program want?

CHAPTER 8

A Real-World Oriented Learning- Facilitation Guidelines

Today's world needs a workforce of creative, curious, and self-directed lifelong learners who are capable of conceiving and implementing novel ideas. Unfortunately, this is the type of student that the Prussian model actively suppresses.

— *Salman Khan*

Now, I know what you are thinking: "Facilitating real-world learning sounds hard!" Yes, it does. We can't just plan out our lessons on the back of a napkin after dinner and walk into class the next day expecting to make a difference. Facilitating real-world learning takes a LOT of planning and work. But it's imperative that we create a learning experience that transforms our students' lives.

But it's a fact that transforming our students into lifelong learners with strong 21st-century skills is like climbing Mount Everest! Yet what other option do we have? This is the emotional labor you and I signed up for, so we ought to do it and keep our promises to our learners that we talked about earlier in this manual, helping them to become better one classroom session at a time.

Since it's hard, maybe real-world-oriented learning-facilitation guidelines are a good place to start. They might help you prioritize cognitive tasks, metacognitive skills, and real-world examples and experiences. And coupled with the right tools and strategies, maybe these learning-facilitation guidelines can help students transform shallow learning into flexible knowledge.

The guidelines are divided into seven sections:

1. Real-Word Teaching Goals
2. Learner-Centered Facilitation
3. Decision-Making
4. Effective Classroom Practice
5. Learning Reinforcement
6. Assessment and Evaluation
7. Learning or Knowledge Transfer

You shouldn't expect to address all the principles in these seven sections in every lesson you teach. But when you plan your module or lesson unit, keep these principles listed under each guideline in mind. They can help you provide instruction and create learning tasks that mimic the real world.

HOW TO ACHIEVE BETTER STUDENT RETENTION

The first section of the guidelines is Real-World Teaching Goals. These nine guidelines are as follows:

Section I- Real-World Teaching Goals	✔
1. Promote deep-structure learning, mastery, and learner autonomy	
2. Transfer classroom learning to real-world situations	
3. Promote a growth mindset, protect students against learning stereotypes, and address self-esteem issues (negative past learning experiences that may prevent learners from doing their best)	
4. Develop speaking or communication skills (regardless of the subject you teach)	
5. Increase reading comprehension skills (summarizing, analyzing evidence)	
6. Develop writing skills	
7. Promote students' critical thinking skills	
8. Increase technology skills	
9. Develop emotional intelligence, self-regulation, and leadership skills	

The second section of the guidelines is Learning-centered Facilitation.

Section II- Learning-Centered Facilitation	✔
1. Start with real-world, driving questions and encourage students to pose additional questions	
2. Pique learners' curiosity (to get them to think about and engage with the content in a deeper way, which will lead to better information retention)	
3. Use an inquiry-based approach to develop thinking skills and use experiential learning to promote learning by doing and reflecting	
4. Make the learning process rigorous (by challenging assumptions and making learners think on their feet)	
5. Avoid giving answers out too freely (so learners instead have to search, discover, explore, and support their thoughts and ideas)	
6. Leverage learners' passion and interest (by affording them space to personalize and individualize their assignments or projects)	
7. Use the content's best modality (the best way to teach a subject) and expose learners to materials in a variety of ways (videos, demonstration, texts, realia, authentic materials and real-life examples)	
8. Create a risk free-environment, but help learners to acknowledge and deal with their fears	
9. Bring experts or other professionals into the class and encourage learners to have their questions answered	

The third section of the guidelines is Decision-Making. There are four guidelines:

Section III- Decision-Making	✔
1. Create space for learners to participate in decision-making and share their opinions, thoughts, and feelings	
2. Give learners time and space to contemplate how they best think, work, and learn (that is, to reflect on identifying key issues, make adjustments and request appropriate help)	
3. Encourage students to create learning products that match their level of readiness, and their personal and career goals	
4. Use learning activities that involve students analyzing and discussing content, negotiating meaning, making joint decisions, and creating products to showcase their comprehension and skills	

The fourth section of the guidelines is Effective Classroom Practice. These nine guidelines are as follows:

Section IV- Effective Classroom Practice	✔
1. Teach how to learn or the best ways to access and practice your content (act like a mentor or a coach)	
2. Build learners' background knowledge in your content area (what are important for analyzing, synthesizing, and critiquing skills)	
3. Promote effective and consistent practice (with intent and free of distraction)	
4. Teach effective study skills (discussing study skills and the best ways to learn and master target content)	
5. Use activities that make learners think deeply about new content and skills	
6. Welcome mistakes and celebrate efforts and hard work	
7. Distribute practice sessions over several weeks (to avoid massed practices or cramming)	
8. Promote collaboration, peer-learning, and value social interactions (teamwork, group discussions)	
9. Avoid idle time and promote healthy breaks	

The fifth section of the guidelines is Learning Reinforcement. There are four guidelines:

V- Learning Reinforcement	✔
1. Use well-designed extension activities or projects to reinforce classroom learning and new skills	
2. Use the case-based learning approach to create opportunities for learners to use critical thinking and analytical skills to work in groups or in pairs on real world challenges	
3. Implement project-based learning activities that mimic the real world (so students solve meaningful and complex problems for a real audience)	
4. Use problem-based learning model to foster classroom collaboration, allowing learners to show critical thinking skills and creativity	

The sixth section of the guidelines is Decision-Making. There are nine guidelines:

VI- Assessment and Evaluation	✔
1. Assess and evaluate students' learning with authentic assessment tools and activities that simulate real-life contexts	
2. Collect and use learners' performance data to make adjustments as necessary	
3. Keep learners informed on how they are doing as it relates to specific standards, goal, or rubric they are supposed to meet	
4. Hold groups and individual learners accountable (using participation rubrics and guidelines)	
5. Provide effective feedback that is timely, corrective, criterion-based, student-facilitated	
6. Use rubrics and guidelines to set clear learning and evaluation expectations	
7. Implement learning/assessment portfolio for all adult students	
8. Promote self-reflection on learning (providing learners with quiet time for that purpose)	
9. Never ask, "Do you understand?" to assess learning, but instead observe performance on concrete tasks	

The seventh section of the guidelines is Knowledge Transfer. These four guidelines are as follows:

VII- Knowledge Transfer	✔
1. Create tasks that allow learners to transfer knowledge learned in class to real-world situations	
2. Motivate learners to work on open-ended problems that require the use of real world-skills	
3. Expose learners to experiences outside the classroom setting (creating opportunities for learners to manipulate content, engage in meaningful discussions, and complete meaningful projects)	
4. Raise learners' awareness on the importance of irreplaceable skills (artistic and soft skills—skills that lead to jobs robots cannot do well or at all)	

When you plan your module or lesson unit, keep the following questions in mind. They can help you think more deeply about how to create instruction that reflects the real world.

1. What are your real-world learning objectives?
2. What are your real-world, driving questions for your students?
3. How and when will students discuss standards?
4. What are the main skills students will practice and master?
5. What real-world stories or examples will you share?
6. How will you trigger your learners' interest?
7. How will you activate prior knowledge?
8. How will learners develop or access new factual knowledge?
9. What key terms or concepts should the learners know?
10. What and how will learners contribute to the lessons?
11. What authentic products will learners create?
12. What rubrics will you use for evaluation?
13. How will you make learners think deeply about content?
14. How will you facilitate or promote independent study time?
15. How will learners use technology to foster learning?
16. How will you differentiate instruction?
17. What learning activities can be used to mimic real-world situations?
18. How will learners reinforce their learning and skills?
19. What opportunity for independent practice will students have?
20. What opportunity for teamwork practice will students have?
21. How much time will be dedicated to discussion?
22. How much time will be dedicated to collaboration or project?
23. What authentic materials will students use?
24. What opportunity for authentic assessment will learners have?
25. How will learners demonstrate critical thinking skills?
26. What speaking or presentation opportunities will students have?

27. How often will learners reflect on the learning process?
28. How will the key skills and content be presented on the test?
29. How will the lessons meet WIOA expectations?
30. How will you measure deeper learning and mastery?

CONCLUSION

Leadership is solving problems. The day soldiers stop bringing you their problems is the day you have stopped leading them. They have either lost confidence that you can help or concluded you do not care. Either case is a failure of leadership.

– Colin Powell

    Now, it's up to you to decide: Do you truly want to be an indispensable team player in adult education? Do you want to make an impact on students' lives? Do you want to teach for real change and keep your promises to your learners?

    This book has encouraged you to take the matter of student retention into your own hands, use your true calling in adult ed, and keep your promises to take learners closer their dreams—helping them become the professionals they desire to be. It has also provided some instructional ideas you can use and adapt to get the job done.

At its core, this book invites you to change from following the status quo. To quote Seth Godin, "Whatever the status quo is, changing it gives you the opportunity to be remarkable."

Now, all that is left is for you to take concrete actions for the benefit of the learners you and your program seek to serve. The options are clear: average versus remarkable. A work of art versus compliance work. I hope you make the best decision—for the sake of your learners who so desperately need your help to face the real world (and the test, too!).

Can you do me a favor? Please help spread the word. If you've learned anything from this book, please give this copy to someone else who can use it. Invite them to read it. Ask them to make a choice about the true calling in adult education. Adult students need them— and their best work.

SOURCES

Adams, S. (2013). *How to Fail at Almost Everything and Still Win Big*: Kind of the Story of My Life. Penguin.

Adult Education and Literacy. (n.d.). U.S. Department of Education. Retrieved from https://www2.ed.gov/about/offices/list/ovae/pi/AdultEd/index.html?exp=6

Adult learner persistent.(n.d.). Evidence-based Strategies – Examples, Research and Tools. Retrieved from https://nelrc.org/persist/counseling_evid_c.html

Collins, J. (2016). *Good to Great: Why Some Companies Make the Leap and Others Don't*. Instaread.

Delisio, E. M. (2002, June 4). What it education today means for you tomorrow. *Education World*. Retrieved from https:/www.educationworld.com/a_issues/issue25.htm

DeNeen, J.(2012, October 15). Holistic Teaching: 20 Reasons Why Educators Should Consider a Student's Emotional Well-Being. InformED. Retrieved from http://www.opencolleges.edu.au/informed/other/holistic-teaching-20-reasons-why-educators-should-consider-a-students-emotional-well-being/

Dweck, C. S. (2008). *Mindset: The new psychology of success*. Random House Digital, Inc..

Godin, S. (2018). *This is marketing: You can't be seen until you learn to see.* New York, Portfolio/Penguin.

Godin, S. (2009). *Purple Cow, New Edition: Transform Your Business by Being Remarkable.* Penguin.

Godin, S. (2008). *Tribes: We need you to lead us.* Penguin. New York

Hardiman, M. M. (2012). *The brain-targeted teaching model for 21st-century schools.* Corwin Press.

Kaiser, H.(n.d.).What Is Problem Solving? MindTools. Retrieved from https://www.mindtools.com/pages/article/newTMC_00.htm

Kerka, S. (1988). Strategies for Retaining Adult Students: *The Educationally Disadvantaged.* ERIC Digest No. 76. Retrieved from https://www.ericdigests.org/pre-929/adult.htm

Kilgore, W. (2016, June 20). UX to LX: The Rise of Learner Experience Design. EdSurge. Retrieved from https://www.edsurge.com/news/2016-06-20-ux-to-lx-the-rise-of-learner-experience-design

Lynch, M. (2018, December 9). 6 Ways Teachers Can Foster Cultural Awareness in the Classroom. *Huffington post.* Retrieved from https://www.huffingtonpost.com/matthew-lynch-edd/6-ways-teachers-can-foste_b_6294328.html

McLeod, S.(2005). Maslow's hierarchy of needs. Simply Psychology. Retrieved from https://www.simplypsychology.org/maslow.html

Willingham, D. T. (2009). *Why don't students like school?: A cognitive scientist answers questions about how the mind works and what it means for the classroom.* John Wiley & Sons.

Willingham, D. T. (2008). What will improve a student's memory. *American Educator*, 32(4), 17-25. Retrieved from https://www.aft.org/sites/default/files/periodicals/wilAutmalingham_0.pdf

Willingham, D. T. (2004). "Ask the Cognitive Scientist Practice Makes Perfect, But Only If You Practice Beyond the Point of Perfection." *American Educator* 28, no. 1: 31-33. Retrieved from https://www.aft.org/periodical/american-educator/spring-2004/ask-cognitive-scientist

Willingham, D. T. (2002). Ask the Cognitive Scientist Inflexible Knowledge: The First Step to Expertise. *American educator*, 26(4), 31-33.

ABOUT THE AUTHOR

    Teddy Edouard has helped educational and workforce institutions create holistic student-centered learning environments that maximize academic and career success for area youth and young adults. He has worked as an academic, administrator, and learning consultant in a variety of programs in not just the DC and Baltimore areas, but nationwide. In addition to this, he has coached instructors in three different countries. He has over 18 years of experience in education and learning design and possesses an MA in Teaching from SIT Graduate Institute and an MSEd from Purdue University. He can be reached via https://coachingforbetterlearning.com/
or at coachingforbetterlearning@gmail.com.

Made in United States
Orlando, FL
01 August 2024

49771588R00046